THE RISE AND FALL OF THE

XFL

& THE 2019 SEASON

MATTHEW MAZZA

PUBLISHED BY FIDELI PUBLISHING, INC.

ISBN: 978-1-948638-02-9

Published by
Fideli Publishing, Inc.
119 W. Morgan St.
Martinsville, IN 46151

www.FideliPublishing.com

TABLE OF CONTENTS

Introduction

As an avid football fan imagine being able to watch football year-round. Especially following the Super Bowl in February, it would be wonderful to continue the great sport of football for the rest of the year.

The discussions in this book, will review the excitement from the 2019 season by reliving some of the best moments during the season, postseason, and Super Bowl. In addition, the book addresses a step by step plan to show the differences between the XFL and the NFL. The discussion of the XFL will show its growth through the rules, teams, and ownership. Also, explaining why the XFL failed in 2001 and it`s revival and failure of the 2020 XFL season.

For millions of football fans around the country it would be a dream come true instead of the season ending with the Super Bowl, allowing football to continue through the XFL which will be a highlight for all fans. The opportunity for the football season to continue well into the spring will allow the fans to follow an additional league. This would be a real triumph for the fans and for the sport itself.

The 2019 NFL Season

The 2019 NFL (National Football League) season was one of the most exciting, enjoyable, and wild rides the NFL has seen in a long while. The NFL celebrated its 100th anniversary during the 2019 season. There were many offseason moves beforehand, these really hyped the fans dramatically. Antonio Brown went to the Oakland Raiders, Le`Veon Bell to the New York Jets and many more.

The year started with Antonio Brown arguing with the Raiders owner, Mark Clark Davis and the Commissioner of Football Rodger Godell which led to him getting cut by the Raiders. Later in the year,

New England Patriots signed Brown and then cut him after just a short time with them. Odell Beckham Jr. found a new home after getting traded to the Cleveland Browns for Jabrill Peppers and a couple of other draft picks. Those were some of the biggest offseason trades and signings, around the league.

The San Francisco 49ers have been identified as one of the worst teams for several years according to statistics. However, in 2019 they became the top seed in the NFC (National Football Conference). Along with the 49ers the Baltimore Ravens were the top seed in the AFC (American Football Conference).

The two teams succeeded in different ways, the 49ers relied mostly on the run game, but when a throw was needed, their quarterback Jimmy Garoppolo was there to fire a bullet pass in a tight window which could be considered an exciting play. Their defense was led by Nick Bosa and fellow pass rushers and Richard Sherman who led the secondary. As for the Ravens they relied on Lamar Jackson their mobile quarterback, he could run and pass for as many yards as anyone in the league. Although both these teams were top seeds only one made it to the Super Bowl.

The Cincinnati Bengals were considered the worst team in the NFL this season according to their record, mostly due to their quarterback problems and their defense. The Bengals started their season 0-11 until finally getting their first win against the New York Jets. After getting their first win against the Jets in week 12 of the season they went on to win one more game to make their record two wins and fourteen losses.

The Detroit Lions had similar problems when their quarterback Matthew Stafford was injured and had to go to back up quarterback David Blough. The Lions started the season with a tie and went on to three wins and twelve losses. The Washington Redskins had a record of three wins and thirteen losses despite drafting Dwayne Haskins. Haskins was a quarterback from Ohio State University, and they also signed quality safety Landon Collins. The team had a tough season, they could not figure it out all year, and it led to their head coach Jay Gruden getting fired.

The New England Patriots won the Super Bowl in 2018 which makes them the reigning World Champions of Football and despite being on top of the world a year ago they had their bumps and bruises along the 2019 season. The Patriots started the year perfect, with a record of eight and zero then went on to only win four more and have a record of 12-4 and lost to the Tennessee Titans in the wildcard to put the end to a long season of Patriot football.

On TNF (Thursday Night Football) to kick-off week 11 the Cleveland Browns hosted their bitter rivals the Pittsburg Steelers. The game was a blow out with the Browns winning throughout the whole game, and when the game was in its final minutes the Steelers had the ball and the excitement started. Mason Rudolph the Steelers quarterback took the snap and suffered a late hit from one of the Browns pass rushers, the offensive linemen stepped in and reacted. After both sides exchanged words it broke out into a sideline clearing brawl. This also included Myles Garrett (Browns defensive end) ripping off Rudolph`s helmet and banging it onto Rudolph`s head. Multiple flags and penalties were given to both sides. After discussing punishments, they suspended Garrett for the rest of the season and possibly next season. After the season was over the NFL decided to reinstate Garrett for the 2020 season. Understanding, this kind of behavior puts a negative view of professional athletes.

The New Orleans Saints have been one of the best football teams, for the past couple of years, making it to the playoffs in 2017, 2018 and 2019. Despite making it to the playoffs three years straight they have not won or made an appearance in the Super Bowl during that span of time.

In 2017, after winning the wildcard they went on to face number two seed the Minnesota Vikings. The Saints struggled to score in the first half and found themselves down 17 to nothing to start the third quarter. After dominating the second half the Saints found themselves winning 24 to 23 with only 29 seconds left in the game. It looked like all hope was lost for the Vikings, however, the Saints were forced to kick off the ball back to them and they had thirty seconds left to try to score. Vikings quarterback Case Keenum marched them to the 39 yard line and had 10 seconds for one final throw, he found the star wide receiver Stefon Diggs and he ran it in for a touchdown to win the game. The play became known as, the Minneapolis Miracle.

One year following the devasting loss, the Saints had everything going right for them, they were the best seed in the NFC. After they won the divisional round against the Eagles, they went on to play the Los Angeles Rams who were the second seed which meant it was going to be an exciting championship weekend. The game was a tightly contested, the Saints were favored the whole time at the Mercedes Benz Super Dome. Toward the end of the game the Saints quarterback Drew Brees threw the ball to a receiver and a defender clearly interfered, while the whole stadium and benches waited for a flag no flag was thrown.

This led to another devasting loss for the Saints. This call influenced the NFL to add a rule, which allowed coaches to be able to challenge a defensive/offensive pass interference call. In the 2019 playoffs the Saints were the number 3 seed and were favored to go far in the playoffs but first they had to compete in the wildcard game against the Vikings.

This was another tightly contested game that ended up in overtime, and once again the Vikings took the ball and scored on a controversial pass interference play, no penalty was called and led the Saints to another devastating loss.

After the season ended, the New York Giants quarterback Eli Manning announced his retirement. Before the season started, the Giants had the sixth overall pick in the draft and they chose a quarterback out of Duke University, Daniel Jones. Despite the fan's criticism, Jones was able to put on an impressive rookie season. Manning started the first two games and lost them both, Jones started every game until week 14 when he had an injury that lasted two weeks.

Manning was able to play against division rival the Eagles and played the following week against the Miami Dolphins. He lost against the Eagles and beat the Dolphins. Manning indicated, he did not like being a back-up nor a coach.

Giants owner John Mara decided that no Giant will ever wear Manning's number ten ever again. Manning's last words with the team during a press conference were, "Once a Giant. Always a Giant. For me, it's only a Giant."

The next question will be, does he get into the Hall of Fame?

Recap of the 2019 NFL Playoffs

In the 2019 NFL season there were many enjoyable moments, there were free agent signings, trades, and great team stories, which was previously described in chapter 1. Twelve teams made it to the NFL playoffs, six teams on the AFC and six teams on the NFC. The teams from the AFC are the Baltimore Ravens, Kansas City Chiefs, New England Patriots, Houston Texans, Buffalo Bills, and the Tennessee Titans. On the NFC side the teams that made it were the San Francisco 49ers, Green Bay Packers, New Orleans Saints, Philadelphia Eagles, Seattle Seahawks, and the Minnesota Vikings.

The 2019 NFL playoffs had some of the biggest and most shocking moments of the playoff season in recent years. Some of these big moments were surprising while others were predictable. It is clear that when the playoffs come around some teams struggle while other teams truly succeed. The playoffs are set up so that the only team to win is the best, as it is considered a "win or go home". Each moment was crucial to having us find out who would play in the Super Bowl.

The AFC wild card weekend had a lot of excitement, starting with the Houston Texans hosting the Buffalo Bills in NRG Stadium. The Texans were trailing Josh Allen and the Bills by 16 at the beginning of the game, but the Texans defense only gave up 3 points while the Texans offense battled up a total of 22 points and claimed the win over the Bills to move on. The second AFC wild card match up were the Tennessee Titans going into Foxborough and beating the heavily favored New England Patriots. This game flipped flop in the first half, the third quarter was scoreless, and the fourth quarter decided it when the Titans took a critical lead toward the end, with Titans winning.

The NFC wild card weekend had similar excitement when it came to the Saints and Vikings game. They were playing in the New Orleans Mercedes Benz Super Dome; the New Orleans Saints were favored against the Minnesota Vikings. However, as discussed in the first chapter the Vikings came in and shocked the Saints on a controversial non call in the endzone to win the game. The battle of the birds kept the second game interesting as the Eagles and the Seahawks put together a great entertaining game to watch. The young star quarterback Carson Wentz left the game with a concussion the Seahawks went on to take the win.

The following week the winners from the wild-card weekend faced the teams with a "bye". The two teams with the "bye" from the AFC were the Baltimore Ravens and the Kansas City Chiefs. The match ups were scheduled to feature the Ravens and Titans on prime-time Saturday night. It was clear that everybody favored the number one seed to beat the Titans who were the number six seed in a blowout game. However, the Titans did not allow that to happen, instead Derick Henry (Titans running back) carried the team to the championship game.

The second game featured the Kansas Chiefs playing hosts to the Houston Texans. This game started with the Texans leading twenty-four to zero going into the second quarter until the Chiefs made three touchdowns scores in three minutes. This flipped the game around completely leading to the Chiefs to go on and win the divisional round weekend.

On the NFC side the two teams with the "bye" were the San Francisco 49ers and the Green Bay Packers. The match ups that took place were the 49ers hosting, the Minnesota Vikings resulting in a pretty uneventful game with the 49ers coming out on top. The other game took place in the very cold Green Bay Wisconsin, between the Packers and the Seahawks. This was a rematch of the 2014 championship round which ended with the Packers winning. This divisional weekend for the NFC resulted in the two top seeds to move into the Championship weekend.

With the AFC divisional round resulting in the Chiefs and the Titans winning, the Chiefs would go on to host the AFC Championship game in Arrowhead Stadium in Kansas City. This game was a very intense game when the Titans silenced the crowd and took a ten to zero lead. Patrick Mahomes and Tyreek Hill from the Chiefs made quick adjustments on the other side of the ball, totally dominating and went on to win and become the AFC Champions.

The NFC game was held in Santa Clara, California in Levi's Stadium, home of the 49ers. This game started with the 49ers winning and they maintained the win, the 49ers dominated the entire game and never really let Aaron Rodgers have a chance at accomplishing anything productive. The San Francisco 49ers became NFC Champions.

Super Bowl Sunday, February 2020 resulted in a great time for fans across the Nation. The Super Bowl was held in Miami, that was the 11th time the Super Bowl was played in Miami. It was the most Super Bowls played in any city in history. As usual, the excitement started about a week before the big game when the media was introduced to the players and they were able to get all their questions answered, before the big Sunday game.

Finally, it was Super Bowl Sunday and fans were hyped around the country picking sides, betting on all sorts of things such as, winner of coin toss, what penalty will be called first, the winner of the game and much more betting took place all before the big game even started.

Now, just after six thirty in the evening eastern standard time. The kickoff started and the Super Bowl was underway. San Francisco took an early lead on their opponent, Kansas City and at this point both sides were happy. The 49ers fans were happy because they never lost a game they started off with the lead (in the 2019 playoffs) and the Chiefs never lost a game without losing by at least two scores (in the 2019 playoffs). The game continued and at this point both sides received their elusive first scores. The 49ers held onto a lead going into halftime.

Following the halftime show, the 49ers maintained a strong third quarter, going into the fourth quarter the 49ers were up twenty to ten and it seemed like they were dominating until Mahomes and his teammates woke up and became very aggressive on the field.

The Chiefs seemed to be sleeping during the whole game, but they dominated the fourth quarter. The Chiefs ended up winning the game by a score of thirty-one to twenty. The Kansas City Chiefs were named Super Bowl 54 World Champions. This Super Bowl will live on as one of the most exciting Super Bowls during this era and allowed for a strong final touch to the 100th anniversary of the National Football League.

NFL Season Ends
& the Rise of the XFL

Following the Super Bowl, the NFL fans usually wait for the scouting combine which is where head coaches and general managers go to Lucas Oil Stadium the home of the Indianapolis Colts. The coaches and GMs get together and watch college players showcase their talent. During this time, the coaches and GMs collect all the analytics they need in order to get a good player from the draft.

A little bit on the draft, every head coach and GM discuss and decide the player they are going to draft (pick). The commissioner Rodger Godell presents every teams pick; the order of the teams is worst to best based on the previous season.

The NFL fans had heard that there might be something new this year instead of waiting for the scouting combine or the draft they would be able to watch a new league called the Xtreme Football League (XFL). Fans had heard that Vince McMahon was going to be attempting a new league, following the Super Bowl, the hype started to become real.

Along with the discussion of things to come, there were many questions. Some of the fan questions were: What is this new league? What would it be like? Is it worth watching? The big question was that not only fans wanted to know but the entire league, Will it succeed?

The questions persisted, however, with a new league following after the NFL they also would have to meet the many expectations of the fans. One of the biggest mistakes the NFL made was in the opinion of many fans, they made too many rules and penalties because fans wanted to say, "Just play the game." One of the biggest expectations of the new league was would it be a league with fewer penalties than the NFL.

The 2001 XFL

The XFL was creating a completely new league, however, the name of the league has been used before. In 2001, there was an up and coming league that was called the XFL and meant the same thing Xtreme Football League. In that league there was a number of things that went wrong along the way.

There was an attempt to make an Eastern United States indoor league, with an attempt to have 10 to 12 teams. In February of 2000 Vince McMahon from the World of Wrestling announced they would launch the XFL in the winter of 2001. In comparison the differences from the XFL and NFL were, instead of a coin toss each team would sprint to where the ball was sitting in the middle of the field and fight for the first possession. Also, unlike the NFL you were not allowed to signal for a fair catch.

The league in 2001 failed for several reasons, the rules did not make enough sense to fans, the attempt to blend football and professional wrestling was unsuccessful, and they did not attract viewers to come or to watch games. The L.A. Magazine called it "The wacky, tacky, controversial, ultimately catastrophic failure of the NFL alternative."

The 2020 XFL and the Teams

In 2020, 19 years later, there was a resurgence of the XFL. The former pro bowl quarterback of the Indianapolis Colts Andrew Luck`s father, Oliver Luck is the CEO and Commissioner of the XFL. The new XFL was founded in 2018 and made its inaugural season in 2020. The point of the new league was not so much to blend football and pro wrestling as was in the past, but more to make it as entertaining as possible. They were planning on allowing coaches and refs to wear mics and letting the players get interviewed in the middle of the game. A real opportunity to involve players during the game.

When you bring back a league practically 20 years later that previously failed there appears to be a variety of differences between the two. The point was to begin with an improved league and not to blend football with pro wrestling, like in the previous attempt but more to provide as much access to the fans as possible, and to make it a quicker game then the NFL.

The biggest difference from the XFL and the NFL are that the referees wear mics so the viewers can hear what they are saying to the players. Along with the refs the coaches are also wearing mics so you can hear how they are coaching their players. Hearing what the refs and coaches are saying is great because the fans are now able to get inside the players heads as well as they are allowed to be interviewed in the middle of the game.

Fans have a great opportunity to have access to players, but in order to make the pace of play go quicker than an actual NFL game, they had to change some of the on-field rules. These changes included, a faster play clock where the NFL gives teams 40 seconds to discuss the play in the huddle, the XFL shaved 15 seconds off and only allows 25 seconds in between plays. In the NFL and XFL when there is an incomplete pass the game clock continues to go on unless you`re inside the two-minute warning. Instead of the NFL`s 3 timeouts per half the XFL only allows 2 timeouts per half.

To make the game safer for the players the XFL changed the style and formation for kickoffs and punts. When they kick off the ball instead of the way the NFL has their team run back and block you after you catch it and have the opponents sprinting toward you. The XFL`s formation is to have the receiving team stand about 10 yards from where the ball is caught and the kicking team to be 5 yards away from the receiving teams' blockers. This prevents the "big collision" because there is more of a chance for the team to block for you.

In order to make the game more interesting for players and more entertaining for viewers they made a couple of rule changes. Some of these include one foot inbounds instead of two, after you score a touchdown you have three options and none of them are a field goal extra point. The first one, is the player must get in the endzone from one of the following 2 yard line for 1 point, 5 yard line for 2 points or the 10 yard line for 3 points. Another rule, change was there is a bigger chance for a comeback when the leading team has the ball inside the two-minute warning, they are unable to run out the clock.

Also, there were changes to the normal overtime, there are 5 rounds when it is the teams turn, they line up at the 5 yard line and they have one chance to score. At the completion of 5 rounds they tally up how many points each team gets. The quickest an overtime can last is if one team scores 3 times and holds the opponent to zero. This is closely related to a hockey shootout.

The XFL has eight teams split into two divisions based on geography. One of the two divisions is the Eastern Division and the other is the Western Division. Each team has home and away jersey`s. The season consists of 10 weeks with no "bye" week. At the end of the season, two teams from each division advance to the XFL playoffs. The two teams from the same division will play each other and the winner will move on to a "bowl game" to claim a championship.

The Eastern Division contains four teams, the New York Guardians, St. Louis BattleHawks, Tampa Bay Vipers, and the D.C. Defenders. Three of the Eastern teams are on the Atlantic Coast. However, the St. Louis BattleHawks were the furthest west out of the Eastern Division they are still the furthest East then any of the Western Division teams.

The New York Guardians are the furthest team North in the Eastern Division. The Guardians play in MetLife Stadium ordinarily home of the New York Giants and Jets. The head coach and General Manager is Kevin Gilbride. The main colors of the Guardians are Black, Grey and Red and when they are playing away games their main color is White.

The animal on their helmet/symbol is a monster that looks like a prehistoric dog that can fly.

Heading Southwest to St. Louis is the home of the St. Louis BattleHawks. They play in "The Dome" formerly home to the Rams when they played in St. Louis (now moved to Los Angeles). The head coach and the General Manager is Jonathon Hayes. The main colors of the BattleHawks are Royal and Navy Blue and Grey. The symbol they use is a sword with a pair of wings. This team is said to have one of the best social media fan bases and taunt opposing fan bases via social media.

Stopping in the Nation's Capital we will see the D.C. Defenders. The D.C. Defenders play in Audi Field a soccer-based stadium that is usually hosting D.C. United. The head coach and general manager is Pep Hamilton. The main colors of the D.C. Defenders are Red and White. The Defenders symbol is a shield with lightning bolts crossing each other and "DC" at the bottom of the inside of the shield.

The team furthest south in the Eastern Division is the Tampa Bay Vipers. They play in Raymond James Stadium normally the home of the Tampa Bay Buccaneers. Their head coach and general manager is Marc Trestman. The main colors of the Vipers Green, Gold, and White. The symbol of the Tampa Bay Vipers is a Green "V" shape with a Yellow interior. Although this team plays in Tampa Bay, the Vipers were originally going to play in Orlando, however, they decided on playing in Tampa Bay.

The Western Division has 4 teams named, the Seattle Dragons, L.A. Wildcat, Houston Roughnecks, and the Dallas Renegades. The Western Division is made up of the four teams west of St. Louis to the Pacific Coast.

In Seattle, the northern part of the United States, their team is called the Dragons they play at Century Link Field which is more commonly known for the home of the Seattle Seahawks. Seattle's head coach and general manager is Jim Zorn. The Dragons colors are Navy Blue, Green and Orange, and their symbol is a fire breathing dragon with Green and Blue body with Orange exterior skin/hair.

Staying on the west coast the L.A. Wildcats play all their games in Dignity Health Sport Park, which is a multi-use facility hosting sports from soccer to football on different occasions. The Wildcats head coach and general manager is Winston Moss. Their main colors are Black, Red and a Light Orange. The Wildcats symbol is a Light Orange "L" and to the right a Red "A".

Making the first stop in Texas is the Houston Roughnecks. The Roughnecks play in TDECU (Texas Dow Employees Credit Union) the home field of the University of Houston. The head coach and general manager of the Roughnecks is June Jones. Their main colors are Red, Navy and Grey. The symbol of the Roughnecks is a White and Blue colored tower with a Red colored "H" built into the bottom of the tower with a Red star on top. This team was the only team with a 100% winning percentage at the end of the season with a 5-0 record.

Making the second stop in Texas and the last stop of this chapter are the Dallas Renegades. They play in Globe Life Park the stadium made for the Texas Rangers of baseball. Their head coach and general manger is Bob Stoops. The Renegades main colors are Black, Red and Light Blue. The symbol for this team is a shadowed man with a Light Blue hat and mask with glaring Red eyes.

Questions
Get Answers

As discussed earlier in the book, instead of waiting for the offseason and the scouting combine/draft/start of the season, the NFL fans had been introduced to a new league which was the second attempt of the XFL. The fans had many questions about the XFL. The answers to some of these questions may not be clear, however, they are discussed in the following chapters.

One of the earliest questions was, what is the XFL? That was a big question around football fans and coaches/players as everyone was anxious to get to know what this league was trying to exactly accomplish and how would it affect the NFL. The most basic answer to the question is, it is an additional football league to occupy the time in between the end and the start of the NFL season.

If you go in depth, the league mainly focused on finding the solution to three core things. The first objective is, playing safer, that is one of the biggest goals. The second main objective is they want to make it a faster game, they felt the NFL games take too long, they wanted to make the games quicker. The third, objective is, they wanted to make sure that the viewer/fan of the league/team are having fun. They wanted the fans to get hooked on watching this league.

The question: What is the XFL? runs into the next question: What would the XFL be like? The answer to that question is basically everything that the league wanted to accomplish to add more excitement, a shorter game, and safer version of the NFL. An average NFL game was about 3:12 and the average XFL was about 2:56. A study from ESPN.com said, that this was, "shorter than an NFL game but 11 minutes longer than the XFL`s goal of 2:45." In my opinion, I really think the XFL accomplished their goals.

Another question the NFL fans had, is it worth watching? Some NFL fans loved it and watched their team play every Saturday/Sunday. Other fans thought this was a fake league that was not "legit," and they did not want to watch it. Understanding that the objective of the league was based on three principals, safeness, fun and quickness they actually achieved their goal. However, the only real answer to this question is that each fan had to make their own opinion.

The final and most important question which is discussed in the last chapter is, Will the XFL succeed?

Those were some of the questions and answers, of the NFL fans had as they were introduced to the XFL. As for NFL fans that transferred over to XFL fans temporarily (until the next NFL season) there were many arguing on who the best fanbase really was. However, since it was only a five-week season there really was no strong fanbase.

The Five-Week Season

O ver the course of the five weeks, the XFL made terrific progress with sales, tickets, and merchandising. The players seemed like they were having an enjoyable season as well. One team managed to go undefeated while other teams seemed to have struggled right out of the gate.

Let`s begin with the undefeated Houston Roughnecks, they played three games at home and two games away. The Roughnecks managed to have a winning percentage of 100% and going an astonishing 5-0 record, which was not only the best in the division but the best in the league. This team scored 5 touchdowns on the ground with their running back, 15 passing touchdowns and 1 defensive score, adding up to 21 touchdowns averaging over 4 touchdowns a game.

The second-best record in the XFL was a 3-way tie all of them being in the Eastern division holding a record of 3-2. The D.C. Defenders shared the record with the St. Louis BattleHawks and the New York Guardians. The D.C. Defenders scored only once with a running back, 5 times passing the ball and two defensive scores. They averaged just over 1.5 touchdowns a game.

The St. Louis BattleHawks have scored 10 touchdowns 5 with a running back, and 5 times passing the ball. They averaged exactly 2 touchdowns per game. The New York Guardians have scored twice with a running back, four times passing the ball and scored twice defensively, averaging over 1.5 touchdowns a game.

Following the 3-way tie with a 3-2 record the next few teams did not have the best start coming out of opening week. The next two teams had a record of

2 wins and 3 loses. The L.A. Wildcats and the Dallas Renegades, both play in the Western Division. The L.A. Wildcats had a couple of really exciting weeks scoring a total of 18 touchdowns, 5 running the ball, an amazing 12 times passing the ball and once defensively. They had the two highest scoring games in the league putting up 39 points in week 3 and 41 points in week 5. That averages out to over 3.5 touchdowns a game.

The Dallas Renegades did not do enough, they only scored 3 times running the ball and 5 times passing the ball and never scored defensively. They averaged over 1.5 touchdowns a game.

The final two teams were the ones that really struggled and could only muster up one win and go 1-4. These two teams were the Tampa Bay Vipers and Seattle Dragons. The Tampa Bay Vipers were quite a team running the ball tallying 6 touchdowns as well as 4 touchdowns through the air and one defensively. They averaged out to over 2 touchdowns per game. The Seattle Dragons have scored 12 touchdowns throughout the 5 weeks 4 running the ball, 7 passing the ball and one defensively. They averaged out to 2.4 touchdowns per game. Those were the records and breakdowns on each team as they played throughout the five-week season.

XFL Players Meet NFL Standards

Although the league played for five short weeks some NFL coaches and general managers were super impressed by the way these players played and they even offered XFL players NFL contracts. These are a few of the biggest contracts given to XFL stars.

There were several teams interested and several teams made offers for these standout players in the XFL. The team that was really impressed by the players were the Pittsburg Steelers. The Steelers went on to add the most XFL players to their roster. Other teams that signed XFL players included the Falcons,

Chargers, Ravens, Vikings, Panthers, Saints, Giants, and the Chiefs.

One of the biggest offers and signing was the Carolina Panthers signed Houston Roughnecks quarterback PJ Walker. He had an amazing couple of weeks leading the only undefeated team in the league. As well as leading the league in passing yards with 1,338 and passing 15 touchdowns. One of the other big signings was the reigning Superbowl Champions the Kansas City Chiefs signed former St. Louis BattleHawks quarterback Jordan Ta`amu. Fans could not have been shocked that some of the XFL players were signed into the NFL after an incredible couple of weeks.

Global Pandemic Changes Sports Worldwide

At the time the pandemic hit there were several sporting events going on, football had already ended. The sports in progress were Hockey, and Basketball. The Baseball season was about to begin. The Basketball season was winding down, they were approaching the playoffs. The Hockey season was also winding down. Baseball was just about to begin and the XFL was only five weeks into their season.

During the early months of 2020, almost, everyone was hearing about Covid-19 a Corona Virus, this was a virus that was spreading rapidly in Asia and the world, with all signs leading to China as the epicenter. There were different theories on how the virus exactly started. America was aware it was routed in China, identified by the World Health Organization. Covid-19 eventually hit Italy extremely hard and made a domino effect throughout Europe hitting and affecting almost every European country.

Covid-19 made its way to Seattle, Washington and infected a nursing home and it continued spread rapidly through the United States. At the beginning when Washington State was the most infected area, the Seattle Mariners decided not to play at T-Mobile Park. However, the Baseball season was delayed indefinitely, as of the writing of this book.

As Covid-19 made its way through the country eventually political officials and the CDC (Center of Disease Control) named New York the epicenter of the virus, specifically the area in Westchester known as New Rochelle. The CDC also finally named Covid-19 a Global Pandemic. Eventually, all non-essential businesses had to close as well as schools. Most schools and businesses resorted to online schooling using Zoom and Microsoft Teams. After several months of "stay at home orders" by the Governors, and the complete shutdowns of cities. The Federal Government decided some less impacted states can start reopening. These openings would be phased in over a period of time.

With the MLB knowing that some states can reopen they started planning out how they could play a season. One thing was for sure, with the social distancing in affect there would be no way thousands of fans could come to games for any sports in the near future. While the baseball season was trying to start both the Basketball Commissioner and the Hockey Commissioner were trying to think of ways to start up their seasons and pick up where they left off.

As for the NFL the season it is over and does not start again until the fall, but this league was impacted as well. The NFL draft decided that it would not be put off or delayed, they concluded that it will be virtual, and the Commissioner Rodger Godell did it live from his New York basement. Although, the NFL draft was different than usual it was the only live/sports related event on at the time and broke records all three nights of the draft. As they plan for the season ahead the league will wait to see where they are in the fall and what the Governors and the CDC says, this is still a very fluid situation.

The book does not discuss all the sports that have been affected but these are some of the American sports that were impacted. It will be interesting to see and watch how they will move forward with all other sports as the seasons approach.

The Fall of the XFL

The XFL was affected in a different way, they had just started their season and they invested a great deal of money into the league. They were the last league to announce that they would be putting the season on hold on March 12, 2020.

After the league put the season on hold for a couple of weeks, they decided to suspend all operations of the XFL and lay off all part time employees until the next season. After a couple days they released a statement, stating, that it would be extremely hard to restart the league this season. This was very disappointing to many fans and owners.

The XFL owners did not want the season to close like this but Vince McMahon announced the league would be filing for Chapter 11 bankruptcy. As well as putting out the statement which they expressed, it would be extremely hard and not likely to restart for a third time. Unfortunately, that was the fall of the Xtreme Football League.

A Final Thought

Finally, the XFL and NFL fans, players, coaches had one last question. This question will linger on for a long time, will the League ever start up again? In the previous chapter it was stated that it would be extremely hard for them to start up for a third time, however, anything is possible. The future of the XFL and Vince McMahon is truly an unknown story and we will just have to wait to see what happens.

Although with Covid-19 there are many questions dealing with the future of sports. The possibility does exist that a new league can get started after the National league finishes their season. This is always a possibility.

Could there be a league during the season? For example, if the XFL did not start when the NFL was finished, and they started during the NFL season. How would this happen? We all know that the NFL plays on Thursday, Sunday and Monday and college football occupies the day on Saturday. Possibly, the second league whether it is the XFL or another league could play on Friday`s?

Those are some of the questions, that have come up in the course of writing this book. It will be interesting to see how exactly these questions get answered. As a sports fan, it will be interesting to think of the questions and answers for yourself.

A Thank You

While writing this book, as the onset of Covid-19 was taking place, it created an abundance of challenging times for everyone. The entire world including the United States has been affected in a serious way. Hundreds of thousands of people have died as a result of Covid-19. Throughout this pandemic we have heard many new phrases we were not familiar with such as, "essential businesses," "stay at home order," "quarantine yourself," "social distancing." These new phrases have become part of our daily life. Having to take extreme measures when leaving our homes, such as, only allowing a limited of people in a store, wearing a surgical mask/face covering, wearing gloves and social distancing of at least six feet.

This book discussed and covered many different athletes and different leagues. With that said, they are nowhere near as essential as the First Responders, HealthCare Workers, and other Essential Workers that were vital in the fight against Covid-19. It should not take a pandemic to thank all the doctors and nurses who cared and spent countless hours doing their job. Also, we need to honor Essential Workers such as, the truckers that deliver our food, the grocery workers that kept the shelves stocked, the farmers that grew the food, and the restaurant employees that prepare the food and all the many others.

I personally know many nurses and doctors throughout my family and friends who have spent a great deal of time recently at their workplace wearing one mask and one pair of gloves all day for a 12+ hour shift. I would like to say, "Thank You".

work that

uring this

ES."

ders,

ntial

ring

About the Author

Matthew Mazza is a 15-year old Sophomore in High School eager to share his knowledge and excitement of sports. He has always had an extreme interest in sports. Primarily football has been his go to sport. However, he acknowledges he is a fan of all sports. Following the Super Bowl excitement of 2019 and the Rise & Fall of the XFL, which prompted him to write this book. He takes the reader on a journey of the 2019 Football Season and the success and failure of the XFL. Matthew has always been a loyal Giants fan and a temporary Guardians fan during the life of the XFL, he is also an avid Yankees fan.

Made in the USA
Monee, IL
17 August 2020

38516426R00036